9 Days
to Heaven

How to make
everlasting meaning
of your life

9 Days to Heaven

How to make everlasting meaning of your life

by
TERESA O'DRISCOLL

This programme will *free you*
from fear and confusion

BOOKS

Winchester, U.K.
New York, U.S.A.

First published by O Books, 2006
An imprint of John Hunt Publishing Ltd.,
The Bothy, Deershot Lodge, Park Lane,
Ropley, Hants, SO24 0BE, UK
office@johnhunt-publishing.com
www.o-books.net

USA and Canada
NBN
custserv@nbnbooks.com
Tel: 1 800 462 6420
Fax: 1 800 338 4550

Singapore
STP
davidbuckland@tlp.com.sg
Tel: 65 6276
Fax: 65 6276 7119

Australia
Brumby Books
sales@brumbybooks.com
Tel: 61 3 9761 5535
Fax: 61 3 9761 7095

South Africa
Alternative Books
altbook@global.co.za
Tel: 27 011 792 7730
Fax: 27 011 972 7787

Text copyright Teresa O'Driscoll 2006
Design: Jim Weaver Design
Cover design: Book Design, London
ISBN-13: 978 1 905047 73 4
ISBN-10: 1 905047 73 8

A CIP catalogue record for this book is available from the British
Library.

Printed by Digital Book Print Ltd

There is a companion 9-track CD available. Each track has
the daily visualisation spoken, natural sounds, and a piece of
meditative music. Please see the website:

www.teresaodriscoll.co.uk.

for more details and more inspiration.

Dedication

To the numerous people I have met over the years who have had little or no experience of God, or who spend no quality time with Him:

'This programme is a direct response to your deep unfulfilled yearning for God making its presence felt.'

And to my mother, Charlotte, father, Thomas, and brother, Ken:

'Through your example of love I have learnt how to love myself, others and God.'

Acknowledgements

Many thanks to Dimitris Zisimopoulos who guided me in the right direction by suggesting the title of the book, then motivated me to send it out into the world.

Thanks also to Joannie Atkinson, Sue Brice, Susan Bruno, Penny Carabella, Gilly Charlemagne, Bob Deakin, Esther Griggs, Sandra Hillard, Brigid Kelly, Reneé and Robert Killian-Dawson, Zeffie Klironomou, Nancy Leff, Astrid Luethe, Janet Parkinson, Artemis Pappas, Sophia Pappas, Doreen Price, Thalia Soteras, Brett Syson, and Mary Xystra, all of whom gave me positive feedback and encouragement; and 'the girls' – Sandra Hill, Bev Lawrence, Kath Wilks and Janet Motto for their great company, caring support and love. And special thanks to my publisher, John Hunt, for the excellent work he is doing in the world, and for his trust in mine.

Warmest thanks to the artist Toni Ndikanwu whose illustrations are brimming with Love.

If you have any questions or comments about this book please contact me at: teresa@teresaodriscoll.co.uk.

Contents

SECTION ONE
The 9-Days-to-Heaven Programme

See life as a journey going either towards God or away from Him. Making a fresh start with God. Expanding the mind to let new ideas flood in.

Considering creation takes you a giant step away from everyday life and that much nearer to God. Opening the channels to Him brings enlightenment.

Meeting with God is easy when you know how. Getting to know Him is a freeing experience. Learning that He already knows and loves you brings peace.

SECTION TWO
The Next Steps

Preface

Are you searching for something lasting to give real meaning to your life, and asking yourself the question 'What's it all about?' If so, your life must be painful in some way.

You may be battling with a major problem, or what feels like an endless series of small ones. Perhaps you are very stressed and wondering if it's all worth the effort. Or, it could be that you are just plain bored with the same mind-numbing routine.

Maybe, you are also living in fear waiting for the next bad thing to happen to you ... or your family, your friends, your pet, your country, the planet, or whatever!

Actually, it is highly likely that whatever is worrying you, fear is at its root, though you may not be aware of that.

Looking at life from the angle of fear it is logical to feel confused. Well, logical to me. Because, of course, I've been there too. And I have discovered that the only lasting thing that switches the light back on for me is to invite God back to the centre of my daily life. Then work through everything with Him.

Because doing this gives me such a wonderfully different perspective on everything, including myself, I wanted to share it with you. And so I have written this book.

It contains a simple, life-changing personal programme. This will open a channel of communication between you and God and take you to His door. After that you will never lose your way again.

This book is for everyone who is interested in God.

In talking to troubled people about God, I have found that they generally fall into one of three categories. Which one is yours? (I am sometimes in the first one.)

1. You already have a strong belief and faith in God but you just haven't been giving Him any quality time lately.
   If so, this programme will bring you closer than ever.

2. You *used* to believe in God but you've 'given up on all that' for some reason.
   Then you will be pleased to discover through the programme that God has definitely *not* given up on you.

3. You don't know God at all and maybe were raised to dismiss even the possibility of His existence.
   If so, prepare to be amazed when the programme proves, through your own experiences, not words, that not only does God exist, He loves you.

No matter which of the categories you fall into (or even swing between) through the programme you will:

- Find lasting peace, happiness and hope
- Be guided to practical solutions to all your problems
- Feel your unique place in the world
- Identify your special talent and how to use it well
- Find the courage to follow your dreams
- Rid yourself of past hurts that are holding you back in the present
- Be equipped to rise to each day's fresh challenge

Walking hand in hand with God daily, your life will be raised above the mundane and into the divine. Through experiencing God this way you will have *everlasting freedom from fear and confusion.*

Being so greatly empowered will enable you to fulfil your destiny and taste immortality. And you will know without a shadow of doubt *exactly 'what it's all about!'*

TERESA O'DRISCOLL 2006

Introduction

Heaven is where God is. God is in you and me and everywhere. We can't see God, so how do we know He exists? The answer is through personal experience.

9 Days To Heaven is a programme that leads the way to a deep experience of God. It does this for an initial nine consecutive-day-period –known as a novena, a powerful spiritual tool.* There will be regular glimpses of heaven on earth as you aim towards an eternity there.

There are many excellent books that are thought provoking, stating the case for God and redemption in words. This little book though, *goes beyond words, to invoke immediate experience of God.*

The nine-day programme is built on the foundation of *The Bible*, Revelation 3:20, 'Behold I stand at the door and knock. If anyone hears my voice and opens the door, I will come in to him and remain with him and him with me'.

To aid concentration throughout the programme you are encouraged to gather nine simple mind-focusing items – such as a small stone (see full list below) – to hold and examine. Some of the book's most important messages are deliberately highlighted by repetition. This will help you to absorb them fully.

---

* Novenas have been used by Christians for thousands of years to pray for special requests. The nine days echo the nine days the early Apostles were instructed to pray for God's help. After that time He sent the Holy Spirit to them.

Collect nine mind-focusing items

The programme will be enriched if you collect together the following nine items and use them as directed each day. They are shown in the order of use.

1. A potted plant
Choose something small and light to pick up and handle easily. One with only foliage is good.

2. A stone
A small pebble with irregular shape, variations in colour, and texture is ideal.

3. A few fresh or dried herb leaves
Choose the one whose fragrance you like best. It could be rosemary, basil, or whatever.

4. A candle
Get a candle in a stable holder. A tea-light is fine.

5. A vial of water
The ideal size and shape is an empty perfume sample filled with water.

6. A packet of sand
A spoonful of sea or builder's sand can be sealed into the corner of a transparent plastic bag.

7. A ring
Use your wedding ring or your favourite dress ring. However, any circle of shiny base metal will do equally well.

8. Some crystal

Choose a small piece or bead of faceted crystal or glass.

9. A vial of perfume

Use a tester of your favourite perfume or after-shave.

Begin to appreciate what you usually take for granted

As you begin to assemble the nine items, use the time as an opportunity to take a fresh look at yourself and your life.

When we want to create anything new and positive the best starting point is to gain a renewed appreciation of what we already have.

Start by simply being grateful when you wake up each day. (If you feel overwhelmed with problems right now, that may be difficult, but do give it a try. It will be worth the effort.) Take a deep breath, wiggle your fingers and toes, open your eyes and look around you. Then flood your mind with gratitude that you can do those things again today.

Being thankful for the gift of a new day, your hands, feet, organs, senses, and so on will set you on the right track towards the counting of blessings.

There is a promise of many more blessings coming your way as soon as you begin the programme.

Become familiar with each item

When you get each item put aside a few minutes to take a good look at it in this way:

1. Pick it up and examine it fully as if you were going to try to draw or paint it.

2. Feel its silent presence. Each and every thing on earth has this. To feel it you need only pay attention to it.

3. Put the item down and as you look at it become aware of the space around it.

4. Now see the space stretching from you to the item. You and it seem to be separate. Fixed. Both are an illusion.

5. Consider the fact that the atoms making up both you and it are in perpetual motion. They are mingling with each other. You are connected to the item and it to you. The whole universe and everything in it is connected. Scientists are studying this connection by means of quantum physics.

6. Close your eyes and put your attention onto your breathing. Don't change it, just observe its rhythm, speed and depth.

7. Flood your mind with an image of your chosen item. In your mind's eye turn it around so that you 'see' it from all angles.

8. Hold that image as you allow your body to relax for a few refreshing moments.

9. When you are ready open your eyes and pick up the item again and acknowledge that you feel a little differently about it now.

Each of the nine items is a symbol

Each item has been chosen as a symbol to trigger a specific positive thought when you see it in your everyday life.

Symbols are an important part of life, whether or not we are aware of it. We see something and without any further thought it holds meaning for us.

For instance, the shape of a heart symbolises love. A cross, symbol of Christianity, is commonly used to show at a glance where help can be obtained, marking say, a humanitarian medical organisation, or a pharmacy.

Without the items

If, for whatever reason, you do not want to collect the nine items together, or do not have the relevant one at hand, you can still do the familiarisations with your imagination.

For later

Later on, you will find that the exercises become even more powerful as you become more familiar with them. Carrying them out with a friend or group of like-minded people could deepen the experiences still further.

You may like to do some of the familiarisations outdoors. Perhaps on a beach and hold a handful of sand. Or in a forest and pick up some leaves from under a tree. Or maybe, in a park and take up a stone from the ground, and so on.

You can record the visualisations and listen to them. **For your convenience there is a companion 9-track CD available.** Each track has the daily visualisation spoken, natural sounds, and a piece of meditative music. Please see the website: www. teresaodriscoll.co.uk for details.

SECTION ONE

The 9-Days-to-Heaven Programme

Some pointers before undertaking the familiarisations

In order for the familiarisations to work, that is, to have in each one an experience of God, it is essential that you truly want to have that experience.

As in every other experience in life you will get out of it to the measure that you put into it.

When you open your heart completely and humbly, and put your whole self and focus into each familiarisation you will meet and commune with God.

Day One –
Opening your mind to God

Set aside about 15 minutes and take steps to ensure you are not interrupted in that time. **You will need your potted plant.**

Life is a journey that can take you either nearer to, or further away from, God and His heavenly home. When your ultimate goal in life is heaven there is an immediate bonus in store for you: the companionship of God every step of the way.

Yes. That is the best news of all!

When heaven is your goal God is always beside you

God does not want to simply wait in heaven for you. He is impatient to be with you right now. Eager to be at your side helping to steer you through every twist and turn of the road. Guiding you at each crossroads.

Though each choice will still ultimately be yours, the comforting nearness of God will add a new perspective to each new situation, dramatically increasing your level of self-confidence.

If you ever feel like something is missing in your life and God is not your target, you can be sure that it is Him. No matter what you achieve. Be it success, wealth, or any other personal goals, life can never be entirely satisfactory without God at its centre.

Only the regular awareness of the presence of God can create the conditions necessary to enjoy real and lasting happiness. Peace. Hope. Joy.

> *Your life is only complete with God at its centre*

Think of today as a fresh chance to start a new and even better way to live life to the full on earth, with regular sightings of heaven, and a clear goal of eternal life with God.

You will take a step closer towards these precious gifts by carrying out the familiarisation that follows shortly. It is a simple way to focus the mind on your choice to grow in the knowledge of God.

It will also put into the spotlight your God-given right to be here on earth.

> *You have a right to be here!*

God is not a stranger to you, but your mind may have been closed for some time, or for as long as you can remember, to His nearness. With a little effort on your part you can build a lasting relationship with Him.

Life will continue to bring challenges daily. However, if you repeat this opening-out procedure regularly it will keep your feet firmly pointed towards heaven.

The instant reward will be soul-felt gratitude of the gift of life.

> *Yes, life is a gift!*

To get the full benefit from anything new it is a good idea to approach it with an open mind. To absorb new information the brain has literally to make new physical connections between its cells.

Hence this mind-expanding exercise. Using this method, the new idea can get past the barriers made up of all of your previous negative decisions and judgements.

Sometimes negative thoughts become a habit. An almost mindless sabotage of your good. From now on, when you catch yourself returning to self-defeating patterns of thinking, take a moment to remind yourself that you can choose another, self-supporting thought to put into its place.

Choose to support yourself with positive thoughts

A plant is used here as a symbol of life and growth. Without vegetation such as your plant there would not be enough oxygen for us to breathe.

In the presence of sunlight the plant takes carbon dioxide from the air through its leaves and changes it into oxygen, which we need to sustain our own lives. When your body has used up the oxygen you breathe out carbon dioxide.

You and your plant are therefore already in perfect harmony.

Familiarisation

1. Put your plant close by. Sit with your back straight.

2. Breathe in through the nose and out through the mouth. Now, starting at your feet, tense up the whole of your body including your face and hands. Hold that tension for a few seconds then release it all, leaving the whole of your body relaxed.

3. Pick up your plant and feel the weight of the pot and the plant. Turn it around in your hands and look at it from every angle seeing the different colours and shapes. Touch the leaves and stems, feeling the differences in texture and form. Put the plant down, sit back comfortably and close your eyes.

4. Now imagine that you are a plant sitting in its pot. Feel your roots growing and beginning to knot up into a ball taking up more and more space inside the small pot. Look at your leaves, they are now starting to wilt or turn brown on the ends through lack of nourishment.

   Take your focus back to your roots. Make the decision to push with them and break through the pot. Feel your roots pushing hard, feel the pot begin to crack, then shatter, and fall off. Push your roots down into the rich soil that surrounds you. Feel them grow quickly and happily in every direction.

   Watch your branches shoot out and be covered in great big glossy leaves and your stem growing so big it turns into a tree trunk reaching towards the sky. Feel the freedom of joining together with the earth and blossoming into that tree.

Open your awareness to God

5. Now feel God beaming sunshine onto your branches
and sending gentle rain to water you, taking care of
your every need. See birds flying to perch and make
nests and take shelter in your branches.

Feel the happiness of being loved, wanted and useful
playing your special role in the natural order of life.

Say aloud a few times the affirmation: *'Dear God, I am
happy just to be alive.'* Continue to repeat this sentence in
your mind for a few relaxing minutes.

Have the intention to remember this feeling of opening
out to God.

Now bring your meditation to a close by saying out loud
just once more, *'Dear God, I am happy just to be alive.'*

Breathe in through the nose and out through the mouth.
Now open your eyes and have a big stretch.

Whenever you see a bird in flight from now on remind yourself that you too are playing your own special role in the natural order of life.

Then say the sentence: *'Dear God, I am happy just to be alive,'* and remember the special feeling of love you just experienced.

Feel the happiness of being loved, wanted and useful.

Day Two –
Seeing yourself as part of God's creation

Set aside about 15 minutes and take steps to ensure you are not interrupted in that time. **You will need your stone.**

Stones have been on this planet since its formation. This makes them a good starting point from which to look backwards to the beginning of creation.

Contemplating this great mystery, when swirling matter turned into natural, self-perpetuating order, takes you a giant step away from everyday life, and that much closer to heaven.

Making a regular shift away from the smallness of daily routine to the grandiose scale of the universe will propel you towards the wider perspective needed to keep letting God in.

> *Switch from the smallness of routine to the grandiose perspective of God*

From this new perspective take a look at *yourself* with a fresh eye and be amazed at the wonder of creation that is *you*.

First of all, acknowledge the miracle of engineering that is your body with all of its functions working smoothly together. Doing such things as regulating your temperature, feeding each cell, and making extra power for you to utilise at will.

Then consider with wonder your senses that permit you to experience your surroundings fully. And the magic of your invisible, yet very real thoughts that enable you plan, talk, work

things out, and choose to put something new into each day.
Marvel at your emotions that pep things up a little, or a lot.

Your body is a miracle of engineering

The eternal parts of you, your soul and your spirit, you may not
be too familiar with as yet. But you will be very soon. It is in
the context of your opening soul and spirit that you will come
to know and embrace ideas, perhaps new to you, that will reveal
the special person you really are.

You will come to appreciate that you have been put here to
participate in, and move forward, a part of God's great plan for
mankind. A plan that centres on our free will to choose a life of
love on earth through God and eternity with Him in heaven.

When you choose love your life has real meaning

Your daily journey towards heaven will, with God's help,
bring enlightenment, as everything you ever wanted to know
about life and the special reason you are here begins to unfold.
These answers, as they slowly but surely start to arrive, will give
greater meaning to everything you do.

Soon you will comprehend fully the true importance of your
personal role in shaping the world's history. This will give you
the courage to turn away completely from old, self-defeating
thoughts of inadequacy and deficiencies. In sharp focus, you
will see your rightful place on earth instead of wondering why
on earth you are here.

You will soon discover exactly why you are here

As you apply the new information about yourself and God to
your everyday life it will add a new dimension, more substance,
to each and every one of your interactions with the world.

With God beside you, love will eventually become an automatic reflex action. In turn you will notice that more love flows towards you. Often from the least expected sources. Loving actions can break down defences and heal relationships quicker than anything else.

Applying love draws more of it into your life

A stone is used here as a symbol of the steadying force of God in your life.

When a builder makes the effort to dig deep and make a solid foundation they maximise the endurance and staying power of the construction.

When you choose to build your life on the foundation stone of God you can be sure that His love will be with you always.

Familiarisation

1. Put your stone close by. Sit with your back straight.

2. Breathe in through the nose and out through the mouth. Now, starting at your feet, tense up the whole of your body including your face and hands. Hold that tension for a few seconds then release it all leaving the whole of your body relaxed.

3. Pick up your stone. Pass it slowly from one hand to the other a few times feeling its weight and temperature as you do so. Turn it over and around a few times, feeling its dryness and texture. Look at the colours, lines, indentations.

4. Now close your eyes and imagine it being formed millions of years ago from gases combining and heating and turning into liquid then cooling and crystallising into this stone.

   Feel the ageless timelessness of the stone you are holding and know with certainty that you are part of this continuum that is eternity. Open out to the knowledge that the Universe, the world, this stone, and you have been designed and created by God.

   Understand that everything fits perfectly into His great plan and that you are a unique and special part of it. Opening your heart to God enables you to receive the guidance necessary to play your personal role in shaping history in accordance with that plan.

Open your heart to God

5. See a golden light flooding over you and recognise that God is the light making a connection between you

and Him. Feel the joy of this precious moment. Now see the light expanding and spreading so that you are completely surrounded by it.

Feel the atmosphere become charged with the vibrations of love.

Now say out loud a few times the affirmation: *'Dear God, you are welcome, I want you in my life.'* Continue to repeat this sentence in your mind for a few relaxing minutes.

Put this feeling of joy into your memory and call upon it regularly during the coming days.

Now bring your meditation to a close by saying out loud just once more, *'Dear God, you are welcome, I want you in my life.'*

Breathe in through the nose and out through the mouth. In your own time open your eyes. Put down the stone and have a big stretch.

Whenever you see a mountain remind yourself that the mountain, the Universe, the world and you have been designed and created by God through love.

Then say the sentence: *Dear God, you are welcome, 'I want you in my life,'* and remember the light and the vibrations of love He brought you.

Recall the special feeling of connection to God.

Day Three –
Setting up a meeting with God

Set aside about 15 minutes and take steps to ensure you are not interrupted in that time. **You will need your herb leaves.**

Talking regularly to God establishes a strong link to heaven which can act as a channel for receiving many wonderful, heart-warming experiences in the here and now, as well as in the future.

Perhaps your decision to spend some real quality time with God is a first for you. The time could not be better spent. You can be sure that this will be the most important meeting of your whole life.

Spending quality time with God is an amazing experience

An ideal place to talk to God is in the tranquil atmosphere created by natural surroundings, such as a forest. Nature provides the natural link to God through His creations.

Each plant, bush, and tree is pulsing with silent, invisible energy. If you open to it you can feel the spirit of each living thing. That can lead you back to a new awareness of your own human nature.

Let your spirit commune with nature's

If you let it, that awareness can strip away your thin veneer of sophistication; the cloak you use to cover your insecurities.

When those insecurities are held up to the light you will notice that most are composed of other people's negative ideas, fears, and limitations transferred to you. It is an unnecessary, heavy burden you carry.

Now that you have chosen to live a life of love you can begin to throw away that load. The resulting sense of freedom will lighten everything in your life.

Choose to live life by your own standards

If you cannot get to a forest or even a park when you want to, you can go there in your mind. Fragrant leafy herbs will help to conjure up the vision of the meeting place.

Having opened your heart, the next step, the meeting, is straightforward. As God, who will never force Himself upon you, is always there waiting patiently, hoping you will seek Him out.

God is waiting for you to speak to Him

When you look for Him, He is there for you. In other words, whenever you want to meet with God you have only to be genuinely open to the possibility of that experience. Then create a quiet time and space in your day and issue the simple invitation: *'Will you please meet with me God?'*

After this meeting today, everything you do, say and experience from this time onwards will be coloured by it.

Speak to God from your heart

When you have shared time with God, and know for sure that you can do this whenever you sincerely want to, nothing the world can throw at you will ever be quite so scary again.

With the removal of fear the new, relaxed you will inevitably begin to treat everything and everyone, including yourself, with greater consideration and respect.

Eventually, compassion will become second nature to you. Caring about what happens to others, including strangers, will prompt you to offer any assistance you can, no matter how busy you feel you are.

People who have known the 'old you' well may be pleasantly surprised at your new approach to life. This can be your opportunity to tell them that you are now living a life of love with God.

Relax into life and be your best loving self

A herb has been used here as the symbol of God's participation in every aspect of your life.

Herbs are freely available for many different purposes. From heightening the flavour of food, healing numerous ailments, to creating a soothing aroma in our homes.

In the coming days and years you will discover the many situations in your daily life that you can invite God to share.

Familiarisation

1. Put your leaves close by. Sit with your back straight.

2. Breathe in through the nose and out through the mouth. Now starting at your feet tense up the whole of your body including your face and hands. Hold that tension for a few seconds, then release it all leaving the whole of your body relaxed.

3. Pick up your leaves and take a good look at them. Look at the variations in colour and the outline of their shape. The little woody stem running from the base upwards that connected it to the plant and drew up nourishment to spread through the leaves.

   Feel the different textures of leaves and stems. Then take one leaf and press it firmly so that it gives off its special and valued fragrance and breathe that in.

4. Now close your eyes and imagine yourself in an old forest that has a thick, soft carpet of the same leaves you are holding, and as you walk on it their fragrance fills your nostrils. It is a warm, sunny afternoon. Take a good look around you.

   See the sunbeams filtering through thick branches. Birds flitting in and out of the trees and low bushes and plants. Hear the twittering sounds they make and their songs to each other. Sit down on the ground with your back against a tree trunk. Lean back with your eyes lightly closed and feel your whole body sink and relax against it.

Open your ears to God

5. Now take your focus to your heart. From your heart ask God to come and talk with you. Tell Him that you want

to get to know Him. Hear God say your name and tell you that He is always there for you.

Feel the warmth of His love surround you and enfold you like two strong arms. Relax back into His arms and feel the peace and tranquillity of His presence.

Say aloud a few times the affirmation: *'Dear God, I am happy to know you.'* Continue to repeat this sentence in your mind for a few relaxing minutes.

Remember this feeling of safety and love and in the course of the coming days, if you begin to get stressed about anything, come back to this feeling.

Now bring your meditation to a close by saying out loud just once more, *'Dear God, I am happy to know you.'*

Breathe in through the nose and out through the mouth. In your own time open your eyes and have a big stretch.

Whenever you see a tree remind yourself that God is always there for you.

Then say the sentence: *'Dear God, I am happy to know you,'* and remember the feeling of peace and tranquillity that His presence gave you.

Feel God's love surrounding and enfolding you like two strong arms.

Day Four –
Opening out to the love of God

Set aside about 15 minutes and take steps to ensure you are not interrupted in that time. **You will need your candle.**

When you do not have a sense of purpose in your life it can feel as if you are walking in darkness. Fortunately, you only have to turn your face towards God to see His guiding light.

This will reveal the way to greater self-worth and higher personal goals as you are filled with the courage to follow your dreams. Putting your focus onto God's love often and beginning to take notice of the many guiding signs He is sending you will take you another step towards heaven.

> *Whatever you focus on increases – let it be God's love*

With God's love you can overcome disappointments and obstacles that would have stopped you in the past. You will move forwards in your life instead of vacillating or dropping back. Now you are ready to claim your goodness, where before you used to sabotage it.

As you begin to surrender into your rightful, God-given role on earth every doubt and qualm you have ever felt about the meaning of life and the validity of your contribution towards the development of mankind will slowly but surely be erased.

> *Your confidence rises as doubts fade*

With God's love working within you will also doubtless feel a new strong sense of personal responsibility towards the world. This may manifest itself in a number of ways.

For instance, where you used to believe that other people or organisations should undertake responsibility for certain problems or issues, you may now want to look for solutions and implement them yourself.

This could be in any area such as the protection of children, the environment, or animals. Whatever good cause you feel strongly pulled towards is the right one for you.

This will take extra effort. However, you will quickly discover that whenever work is done with love, not only are you adding light to the world, but also your personal zest for life increases.

Helping others makes you feel great

When you actively use love in your daily life you will no longer feel a need to push or manipulate situations or others to achieve what you want. Order will come out of chaos, harmony out of discord, and clarity where there used to be confusion.

Love will also make you more aware of when people are trying to manipulate you. Through God's strength, your own strength has increased so you don't have to let that happen anymore.

Love is a positive force

Manipulation can take many forms. Keep alert for its negative presence. For instance, when you look around you with God at your side, you may start to notice the very many ways – some subtle, others blatant – in which people without your experience are trying to wipe out the very name of God from our lives, as if 'God' is a bad word. As if His love is a threat of some sort. That is a very real form of manipulation.

Unfortunately, some people, the ones who are still walking in darkness, would prefer that you and everyone else, stay in the darkness too. Sending them love is the best thing you can do.

Overcome hatred with love

This candle, with its small cheerful flame, is used here to symbolise the inner glow of confidence that God's love brings.

Though in the western world we are blessed with instant electricity, lighting candles is still favoured by many to create the right mood. They are also used to make an occasion special. Be it to make wishes on birthdays, vows at Baptisms, or romance at dinner.

Feel your new relationship with God kindling a warm flame of love within you.

Familiarisation

1. Light your candle, put it safely but close by. Sit with your back straight.

2. Breathe in through the nose and out through the mouth. Now, starting at your feet tense up the whole of your body including your face and hands. Hold that tension for a few seconds, then release it all leaving the whole of your body relaxed.

3. Pick up your lit candle. Feel the weight of candle and holder and the warmth of its flame. Look at that flame. See the way it is formed – the blue of its base surrounding the burning wick. A white tongue reaching upwards from a pale grey centre. A halo of light echoing the outward shape, and so on. When you have examined it in detail put it down safely.

4. Now close your eyes and in your mind's eye see it still burning, its warm flickering glow lighting the darkness of your inner world.

   Feel connected to your ancient ancestors through the timelessness of this flame. See them stretching back from your parents, grandparents, great-grandparents and so on, back to the beginning of mankind. Understand that everything that happened to them before your arrival has led up to this moment.

   There is nothing random about where you have been born or to whom. You are exactly where you are meant to be and you have come here for a reason. You are on earth to carry forward a part of God's plan of love in the way that only you can.

Open up to God's love

5. Take your focus to your heart. Feel it filling with the love of God. Feel that love expanding and spreading out through the whole of your body and from you out to fill the whole of the world.

Feel your rightful place in the spreading of God's love through you.

Now say aloud a few times the affirmation: *'Dear God, please guide me every day of my life in the ways to send your love out to others.'* Continue to repeat this sentence in your mind for a few relaxing minutes.

Remember the love of God filling the whole world through you and recall that joyous feeling regularly during the coming days.

Now bring your meditation to a close by saying out loud just once more, *'Dear God, please guide me every day of my life in the ways to send your love out to others.'*

Breathe in through the nose and out through the mouth. In your own time open your eyes and have a big stretch.

Whenever you see a lighted candle, remind yourself that God is Love.

Then say the sentence: *'Dear God, please guide me every day of my life in the ways to send your love out to others,'* and remember that you have been born for this.

Feel your rightful place in the spreading of God's love through you.

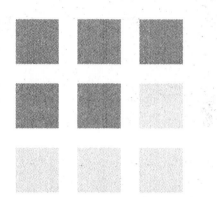

Day Five –
Telling God your fears and problems

Set aside about 15 minutes and take steps to ensure you are not interrupted in that time. **You will need your vial of water.**

Making a promise to yourself to trust and confide in God regularly will take you further towards heaven.

God wants you to ask for His help. He is never too busy to listen to you, and His patience and love for you have no end. They flow out to you as soon as you call His name, just like a living stream of water.

So whenever you feel scared or have a problem that you can't seem to find the answer to, turn to God. He's always there, waiting to take your burden onto His own shoulders for a while.

Sometimes that in itself will be enough to raise your spirits and get you through the worst. Just knowing that you are not alone in your time of need can be a great comfort.

God is never too busy to help you

With God at your side you can face your fears. Fear often makes us blow even the smallest things out of all proportion to the reality of a situation. Quickly we make a jump to imagining the worst-case scenario. So the sooner you bring the balance of God into the equation the better.

When you have tried this a few times and seen that it always works you will begin to call on God first.

When you feel scared call on God immediately

Even when you are walking with God, life will still bring up issues for you to sort through. We are here to grow in love and these challenges are to help us do that.

Try thinking of difficulties as opportunities to increase your capacity to love. When our trials are very hard remembering that and acknowledging it can be the greatest part of the challenge.

This may well be a completely new way for you to view things. It might take some getting used to. You may even find it hard to accept. The best way to banish any doubt is through personal experience. You have already learnt that over these last few days whilst experiencing God.

Through applying love, hardship can be turned into opportunity

When a problem comes up, try asking the question: '*Dear God, please show me how to grow in love through this experience.*' God will always show you the way to love when you let Him. It will then be up to you what you do with His answer. He can only guide you. You will have to take the steps.

Sometimes you will simply have to accept a situation. Other problems will need your input in sorting out. It may not be immediately obvious which is which. This is where God can help and guide.

Ask God to show you how to be loving

As you overcome fears and problems more easily and readily, this will empower you. Your greater energy can be put to good use. Perhaps to help others as you have been helped by God. You will probably find that people begin to ask for your help more than ever before as they feel the positive changes in you.

As you grow in love you will want to help others

Water is used here as the symbol of God's unending love for you.

All civilisations have begun close to a water supply. Being able to obtain a steady supply by simply turning on a tap is one of the major advantages of the western world in the twenty-first century and one which we often take for granted.

However close you come to God, make yourself a promise never to take Him for granted.

Familiarisation

1. Put your vial of water close by. Sit with your back straight.

2. Breathe in through the nose and out through the mouth. Now, starting at your feet, tense up the whole of your body including your face and hands. Hold that tension for a few seconds then release it all, leaving the whole of your body relaxed.

3. Pick up your vial of water and feel the weight of the water and its tiny container. Now gently shake the vial back and forth and watch the water move. This clear, clean liquid is an essential part of our daily life. Without fresh supplies, life would become intolerable. If there were none to be had at all, we would quickly die.

    This precious liquid that we take for granted falls drop by drop from the skies, rushes down mountainsides, and collects as rivers that flow into seas. Along the way we, and nature, use as much of it as we need.

4. Put the vial of water down. Close your eyes and imagine the journey of that water from its arrival as a splash of rain onto a rocky incline. See it joining up with more rain and forming a waterfall.

    The rain stops and warm sun appears. See yourself walking in the sunshine on a green slope towards your waterfall, which is filling a small stream.

    Feel the grass short, springy, and dry under your feet as you take each step. Sit down comfortably on the grass. Take a rest as you listen to the tinkling water running into the stream.

Open out to God's help

5. Feel God arriving to speak with you and hear Him say your name and ask you to call on Him whenever you have a problem and need some assistance in finding a way through it.

Often His answer will be one that you hadn't even considered yourself. Yet you will find it the most appropriate in the circumstances. Feel a sense of relief just knowing that you don't have to deal with everything alone anymore.

Now say aloud a few times the affirmation: *'Dear God, whenever I have a problem please guide me to the solution.'* Continue to repeat this sentence in your mind for a few relaxing minutes.

Remember the feeling of relief that you are not alone with your problems and if anything is worrying you, ask God to guide you through it and come back to this feeling.

Now bring your meditation to a close by saying out loud just once more, *'Dear God, whenever I have a problem please guide me to the solution.'*

Breathe in through the nose and out through the mouth. In your own time open your eyes and have a big stretch.

Whenever you see running water, remind yourself that God wants you to call on Him when you need something.

Then say the sentence: '*Dear God, whenever I have a problem please guide me to the solution,*' and remember the feeling of relief you had when you understood that you are never alone with your problems.

Remember the feeling of confidence that God will show you a solution.

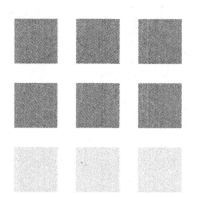

Day Six –
Opening out to your God-given talents

Set aside about 15 minutes and take steps to ensure you are not interrupted in that time. **You will need your packet of sand.**

Sand, just like human beings, is made up of millions of seemingly separate entities that live together and share a similar fate.

Sand is buffeted about by the whims of nature, just as at times each one of us feels pushed around by life and its problems and dilemmas. However, unlike those grains of sand we do not have to just lie there and take what comes.

You always have a choice. Don't see it? Ask for God's guidance

God has given us life and the means to sustain it through the air that we breathe, water and sunshine and plant life. (Some places currently have more of these gifts than others creating an opportunity to physically demonstrate love through sharing.) But more than that, He has given each of us a special talent which, when used wisely, will help us to grow in love and move even closer to heaven.

Your instant reaction to that statement may be to reject it, declaring that you are not talented at all. However, before you dismiss this claim understand that talents can take many forms.

You have definitely got talent

As an exercise, try writing down the things you love to do, enjoy doing and are good at. These are your talents.

Looking at things from this angle you may recognise that you are a gifted teacher, cook, gardener, computer programmer, or whatever.

It could be that you just take that gift, or talent, for granted, or place no value on it. However, if you begin to be grateful for the gift and ask God for guidance on the ways to use it more wisely and with love, it could change your whole life for the better, and subsequently the lives of others too.

Ask God to show you your talent and how He wants you to use it

If your talent is still unclear, God will help you sort out precisely where it lies. He may already be prompting you to sample a new activity or pastime but you keep putting it off. Remembering the old adage, 'You don't know what you can do until you try' follow your instincts; that is, God's guidance. Who knows, it may reveal a hidden natural ability. Or be a step towards it.

Your talent may be beckoning you

If you still can't get a handle on your talent the clue may lie in the way people interact with you. Do they readily confide in you? Ask your advice with their problems? Want you to intervene when they fall out with someone? This could indicate that you have been blessed with a great deal of common sense. Or that your listening skills are excellent. Or that you are a born peacemaker.

Talking this over with your friends or family, if they are perceptive, could bring clues of your talents to the surface.

Bear in mind that whatever your talent is it will be something you love to do.

It could be that you have more than one talent which, when used together and put with your life and job experiences so far, add up to a new career path.

Your talent will shine the way to your unique part in God's plan. When you have discovered what it is, ask Him to help you to put it to the best possible use.

Whatever your talent pray to use it wisely

Sand is used here as the symbol of God's patience with us.

Sand, like the human race, evolves. It has taken aeons to form, though the sea is always adding to the mixture. Our personal evolution in love is also a slow process. Yet we can achieve it with God's help, which He never withholds.

Try to be as patient with yourself and others as God is patient with you.

Familiarisation

1. Put your packet of sand close by. Sit with your back straight.

2. Breathe in through the nose and out through the mouth. Now, starting with your feet, tense up the whole of your body including your face and hands. Hold that tension for a few seconds then release it all, leaving the whole of your body relaxed.

3. Pick up your packet of sand and move it from hand to hand feeling the weight and looking at the thousands upon thousands of grains that make up the contents. Look at them closely and try to identify all the colours of the rainbow that are lying together somehow, giving an overall appearance of beige. Squeeze the packet and feel the tiny hard grains rub together in a soft mass.

4. Put the packet down and close your eyes. Imagine yourself walking on a beach on a warm sunny day. The sand is soft beneath your bare feet, a gentle breeze, tangy with salt, cools your skin and lifts your spirits. Close by you see a big rock jutting out of the sand. Make your way to it and sit down on it facing the sea, which stretches far and wide.

Enjoy God's company

5. Ask God to come and sit beside you so that you can enjoy a few peaceful moments together. Feel His presence as you gaze at the water and watch how the colour changes from deep blue, to pale blue, to white as the tide rushes onto the shoreline. Then leaves behind only a glistening wetness as it recedes for a

few seconds. Listen to the whoosh as it arrives and the sucking of the sand as it departs.

Hear God telling you that you are indeed special and unique. If you know what your talent is begin to ask Him on a daily basis how you can put it to use as part of His plan.

If you haven't yet discovered your talent, make a decision now to talk things over with God very soon and to listen closely for His answers.

Now say aloud a few times the affirmation: *'Dear God, please show me my talents and how to use them wisely.'* Continue to repeat this sentence in your mind for a few relaxing minutes.

Remember feeling special in God's eyes and in the coming days, if you begin to doubt your own abilities, remind yourself that you are now open to finding your unique role in His plan and come back to this feeling.

Now bring your meditation to a close by saying out loud just once more, *'Dear God, please show me my talents and how to use them wisely.'*

Breathe in through the nose and out through the mouth. In your own time open your eyes and have a big stretch.

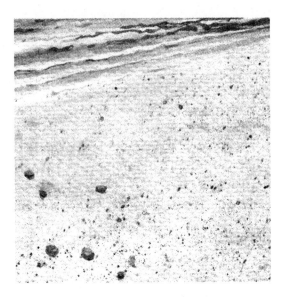

Whenever you see a beach remind yourself
that you are special and unique.

Then say the sentence: *'Dear God, please
show me my talents and how to use them wisely.'*
and begin to watch carefully for His clues
and guidance.

Feel your confidence in life and your
abilities increasing.

Day Seven –
Seeing God within the circle of love and life

Set aside about 15 minutes and take steps to ensure you are not interrupted in that time. **You will need your ring.**

Life only works properly when we treat others as we want to be treated, sometimes referred to as the 'golden rule' or else, 'what goes around, comes around.' Doing this takes us a big step towards heaven.

It is also a simple truth that if we learn to treat ourselves with love, understanding and respect, we will begin to treat everyone else, including God, that way.

We can only love others properly when we love ourselves

By now, as your experiences of God are building one upon the other, it must be becoming virtually impossible for you to deal with people in the same way as the old you used to.

You are probably finding, for instance, that you can no longer impatiently brush off a request that you know you can fulfil with just a little of your time. That you are more tolerant generally with those around you. That things that used to make you mad don't bother you anymore. That your old prejudices are sprouting wings and flying away.

These are all signs of the love of God growing within you.

As that love expands it is impossible to keep it hidden. Its very nature will break through every barrier you have erected between you and others replacing, 'It's not my concern,' with, 'I care. How can I help?'

As love blossoms it cannot be withheld

You may still sometimes find yourself falling back into your old impatient, judgmental pattern of behaviour. At those times try to remind yourself that you are working with love now, and get back on track as quickly as you can.

Expect your love to be tested

As the days go on, start to actively look for ways in which you can be of more use to others than formerly. Doing something without even being asked is a great way to show love.

Even better is doing something useful or kind for someone – be it a stranger or a loved one – without them or anyone else finding out it was you. That way you are demonstrating pure unconditional love.

Unconditional love does not look for the reward of recognition. That it is yours and God's secret is enough. Don't be surprised though by the knock-on effect. Love flooding your unselfish heart may well give you an amazing natural high!

Try doing good anonymously

Everyone will benefit from the new you, especially *you*. The positive gains will be recognisable from the visible improvement in your physical appearance – loving people have a certain glow about them.

Your health too will be better as you stop squeezing up your lymphatic system with the stress of having, for example, to be right all the time. Plus, when you begin to choose not to feel anger and impatience the new calmness in you will greatly reduce the chances of your succumbing to debilitating illnesses.

Your focus on love lights up your inner and outer world

Although you are now experiencing God daily perhaps you are only comfortable speaking to Him when you are alone. But you could try to call on Him when you are at your busiest and most stressed, as even a few seconds of God can be amazingly refreshing.

Just a brief, 'Hello, God,' can be enough to make the connection. That may be all it takes to gain instant perspective as you realise that in the context of everlasting life in heaven with God whatever you are dealing with right now can be got through.

A quick word with God brings perspective to the busiest situation

Here a ring is used as a symbol of the circle of love and life.

For love to flourish and feed the soul it needs to be in constant circulation. Around us. Within us. From God. To God. From us to all of God's creations. And from God's creations to us.

Begin to ask God's help to show you the ways to demonstrate love to everyone you meet.

Familiarisation

1. Put your ring close by. Sit with your back straight.

2. Breathe in through the nose and out through the mouth. Now, starting with your feet, tense up the whole of your body, including your face and hands. Hold that tension for a few seconds then release it all, leaving the whole of your body relaxed.

3. Pick up your ring and pass it from hand to hand a few times to feel its weight. Slip it onto a finger or over a fingertip and feel how it holds you snugly. Move your finger around and see the ring glint in the light. Twist the ring around and around on your finger and see that it has no beginning or end, just like eternity.

4. Now close your eyes and with your imagination see the complete circle of the ring glinting in a beam of sunlight.

   See yourself on a busy street. People rush past you and some almost collide with you, seemingly oblivious of your presence.

Open out to feel connected with God

5. Feel God's hand in yours and instead of getting annoyed remember that you are doing your part in spreading His love out to the world.

   Smile at the people that would have irritated in the past, and ask God to send His blessings to everyone in the world.

   Feel the love you have sent out through God to others returning to you in the circle of life and love, its peace and joy now even stronger.

Now say aloud a few times the affirmation: *'Dear God, please remind me to be this loving way at the most stressful times in my life.'* Continue to repeat this sentence in your mind for a few relaxing minutes.

Remember this feeling of peace and joy and in the coming days if you begin to feel stressed come back to this feeling.

Now bring your meditation to a close by saying out loud just once more, *'Dear God, please remind me to be this loving way at the most stressful times in my life.'*

Breathe in through the nose and out through the mouth. In your own time open your eyes. Put down the ring and have a big stretch.

Whenever you are being jostled in a crowd remind yourself that when you send out love it increases the supply of love within you.

Then say the sentence: '*Dear God, please remind me to be this loving way at the most stressful times in my life,*' and choose to smile at the strangers instead of scowling.

Remember the peace and joy of God's presence in the circle of love and life.

Day Eight –
Forgiving yourself and others

Set aside about 15 minutes and take steps to ensure you are not interrupted in that time. **You will need your crystal.**

Let the rainbow sparkle of pure, clear crystal remind you of the ray of hope always radiating within you from God's love.

This hope though, can often be buried beneath layers of old pain.

In order to go forwards into a bright and hopeful tomorrow, it may be necessary today for you to let go of the past hurts and disappointments of all your yesterdays.

> *Don't let old painful experiences continue to drag you down*

This spiritual healing will enable you to make the most of your new life with God.

Admittedly, it is not always an easy thing to achieve. Especially if you are filled with guilt or holding resentments against others. However, even being willing to begin this healing process will take you another step towards heaven.

> *To begin to release old pain you only need to be willing*

Sometimes past pain is so deeply buried that we may not be consciously aware of its continuing presence. Clues to its existence can be seen though in exaggerated reactions to seemingly minor situations.

If, for example, you are feeling good then suddenly find yourself getting very agitated or emotional when someone makes a throwaway comment to you, it could well be an indication of a raw nerve directly stemming from the pain of a past experience.

Spending a few minutes alone with God, asking His help to backtrack, can dig up the real problem.

Old hurts often stem from painful childhood experiences and when we examine them with the eyes of an adult we can usually ease the hurt with the insight of our added years of knowledge of human behaviour.

Perhaps forgiveness is needed either for yourself or others. With God's assistance, even the deepest hurt can gradually ease when you are simply willing for it to happen.

Take time with God to unearth and release past pain

If the experience was a very bad one it may take some time for the forgiveness to flow. It is worth every bit of effort on your part to bring this about.

The key to release is recognising that, as you are the only one thinking in your head, you alone are the one continuing to hurt you.

Yes. You are hurting yourself. Do you really want to keep doing that? Of course not.

Repeatedly talking things over with God will hopefully enable you to eventually tap into the love and forgiveness that are always in your heart. The relief of letting grievances go can be blissful.

Letting old grievances go can bring bliss

In the present, try to avoid creating new bad situations with people that will lead to pain for either of you. Let your new path of love show you the way to harmony whenever possible.

If some people begin to grate on your nerves you may decide, after talking it over with God, that it is better to keep away from them for a while. Maybe in a few hours, or days, things will improve.

When you come from a state of love though, it is usually possible to see another person's point of view quite quickly. You don't, of course, always have to agree with someone else's opinions.

Strive for harmony within and around you

Crystal is used here as the symbol of the healing force that God's love brings to our lives.

When dull crystal is polished, its sparkle is unleashed. In like manner when healing forgiveness flows into your soul, it cleanses it and liberates the sparkle of hope and love.

If you cannot feel that immediately, remind yourself that your new reality is that God is now helping you to carry all your burdens.

Allow the knowledge of the continual presence of God's love to sink deeply into your being. In that way, forgiveness for self and others will inevitably flow more freely.

Familiarisation

1. Put your crystal close by. Sit with your back straight.

2. Breathe in through the nose and out through the mouth. Now, starting at your feet, tense up the whole of your body, including your face and hands. Hold that tension for a few seconds then release it all, leaving the whole of your body relaxed.

3. Pick up your crystal and weigh it in your hands and notice its cool touch on your skin as you pass it back and forth on your palms. Hold it up to the light until you see a rainbow of colours flashing off its edges.

4. Now close your eyes and see those flashing colours form into an arc of a rainbow high in the sky made by beams of sun shining onto gentle raindrops.

Open out to the comforting nearness of God

5. Ask God to come and sit with you and watch this phenomenon together. Use this opportunity to begin to unburden your very soul.

   If you feel guilty about something make the decision now to forgive yourself. If you feel you have hurt someone, decide now to tell them you are sorry. If, for any reason, it's not possible to be in touch with that person, ask God to pass on the message.

   If someone has hurt you, ask God to give you the strength in the coming days to forgive them. And when you have done that ask Him, if necessary, to pass on the message that they are forgiven to them.

   Feel God giving you a big hug and hear Him telling you that He loves you and is proud that you found the courage to forgive yourself, or to look for forgiveness in your heart towards someone else.

Feel a huge weight begin to lift off your shoulders and a lightness of hope and happiness take its place. Understand that you are now walking on the path of love. Make a pact with God that you will not let anything or anyone turn you away from this everlasting love.

Now say aloud a few times the affirmation: *'Dear God, please walk along the path of love with me all the days of my life.'* Continue to repeat this sentence in your mind for a few relaxing minutes.

Put into memory this feeling of lightness, hope and happiness, and in the coming days, if you begin to feel guilt or resentment, remind yourself that forgiveness sets your feet on the path to love, and come back to this feeling.

Now bring your meditation to a close by saying out loud just once more, *'Dear God, please walk along the path of love with me all the days of my life.'*

Breathe in through the nose and out through the mouth. In your own time open your eyes. Put down the crystal and have a big stretch.

Whenever you see a rainbow remind yourself that God will always give you the strength to forgive.

Then say the sentence: *'Dear God, please walk along this path of love with me all the days of my life,'* and remember that forgiving yourself and others frees you to live your life fully.

Feel the lightness of hope and happiness as you walk on the path of love.

Day Nine –
Putting God into your everyday life brings heaven down to earth

Set aside about 15 minutes and take steps to ensure you are not interrupted in that time. **You will need your vial of perfume.**

Perfume, the distilled essence of flowers, sunshine, rain and air, touches the senses and lifts the spirits. Similarly, inviting God to share in your daily life will enliven and sweeten it enabling you to rise above the mundane and into the divine.

As you surpass mere existence and really live in each moment, you will come near to heaven and also catch regular glimpses of heaven on earth.

Say '*Hello*' to God as soon as you wake, and frequently during the day. As God is love you can catch sight of Him regularly.

Invite God to share your life

Begin to look around you with renewed interest and notice the many acts of love that you encounter: A smile, a mother kissing her baby, kindness, respect, a shoulder to cry on – there are endless ways that love reveals itself.

Start to praise God by applauding His creations such as a bird in flight, or a blazing sunset over an ocean, and you will understand that you are already witnessing flashes of heaven.

As your goal of heaven naturally rises above all your other ambitions you will have increasing experiences of Paradise.

*Praise God's creations and see them as flashes
of Paradise*

You will also begin to feel more and more desire to pass on to others your personal experiences of God.

If you feel a need to speak to someone about Him, do so. Do it gently though. Always bearing in mind any past reservations of your own.

Resist, as far as humanly possible, being drawn into arguments about the existence of God or His relevance today. If someone is genuinely interested, speak your truth quietly. Tell them about your experiences and how they came about.

Explain that if they want to know if God exists or not, they need only to be truly open to experience Him. After you have spoken to such a person remember them in your talks with God.

Be prepared for meeting an increasing amount of such searchers. That is the way of things. People will be drawn to your newly flourishing spirit and soul.

*Be ready to talk about your love of God to
others*

Don't be surprised if you yourself though, experience the occasional sudden doubt about everything you have learnt recently through God.

Low self-esteem, for instance, may unexpectedly resurface and catch you unawares. Or prejudice may take a fierce hold of you when you least expect it.

Do not waste time trying to analyse these lapses. They are a normal part of human growth, especially where the growth concerns love.

Just keep asking God to be with you and help you, and you will come through each test of the strength of your love with flying colours.

Remind yourself at all times that you have a God-given right to be here. You are a unique and special person doing something in God's plan that only you can do. And keep your sights firmly set on Him and heaven.

Sudden doubt is normal! Tell God all about it

Perfume is used here as the symbol of God's invisible, yet very real continual presence in our lives.

Though the rich colours of the flowers are no longer apparent in the liquid, their scent reminds us of their physical beauty.

Begin to regularly pause for a few seconds throughout each day in order to become aware of God's nearness.

Familiarisation

1. Put your vial of perfume close by. Sit with your back straight.

2. Breathe in through the nose and out through the mouth. Now, starting with your feet, tense up the whole of your body including your face and hands. Hold that tension for a few seconds then release it all, leaving the whole of your body relaxed.

3. Pick up your perfume, take out the stopper and breathe in the fragrance deeply. Replace the stopper and put the vial down.

4. Close your eyes and imagine the colour of the flowers that gave up this scent. See them growing in abundance in a small field at the centre of heaven lit by a soft golden light. A gentle breeze wafts their perfume to you.

Taste Paradise

5. Hear God invite you to come and sit with Him for a while in Paradise. Feel the air charged with the love that you have been experiencing together recently.

    Now see a man approaching slowly. He reaches you and extends his hand towards you. As you reach out and grasp his hand you hear God say, 'This is Jesus, my beloved Son. Listen to Him.'

    You feel His hand in yours – strong, cool and steadying. As you gaze at each other you become aware that you have shared many similar experiences. You know that He has suffered all the bad things you have suffered in your life, such as loss, rejection and humiliation, as well as physical pain.

You feel an empathy pass between the two of you.
Then you hear Jesus say, *'I am The Way to heaven.'*

Now say aloud a few times the affirmation: *'Dear God, please help me to follow the footsteps of Jesus to heaven.'* Continue to repeat this sentence in your mind for a few relaxing minutes.

Remember this feeling of empathy with Jesus and if you ever begin to feel overwhelmed by problems remember His strong, steadying hand in yours and come back to this feeling.

Now bring your meditation to a close by saying out loud just once more, *'Dear God, please help me to follow the footsteps of Jesus to heaven.'*

Breathe in through the nose and out through the mouth. In your own time open your eyes and have a big stretch.

Whenever you see some flowers remind yourself that God and Jesus and heaven are always close by.

Then say the sentence: '*Dear God, please help me to follow the footsteps of Jesus to heaven,*' and remember the air charged with love when you met together in Paradise.

Feel the confidence of God's and Jesus' unending love for you.

Summary

This mind map (*see next page*) outlines at a glance each of the nine days of experiences of God and their logical progression from letting Him into your life to making His presence an increasing part of it.

The map also reveals that the thread binding the whole book together is unconditional love for self, others and God.

All loving relationships need quality time to keep them alive and vibrant. So, keep putting aside some time for yourself, others and God.

When you have completed Day Nine of the programme the next logical step is to go back to Day One to begin all over again.

Why this regular new beginning? The answer is that it will keep the goal of heaven firmly in your sights instead of letting it sink back into the mire of good intentions.

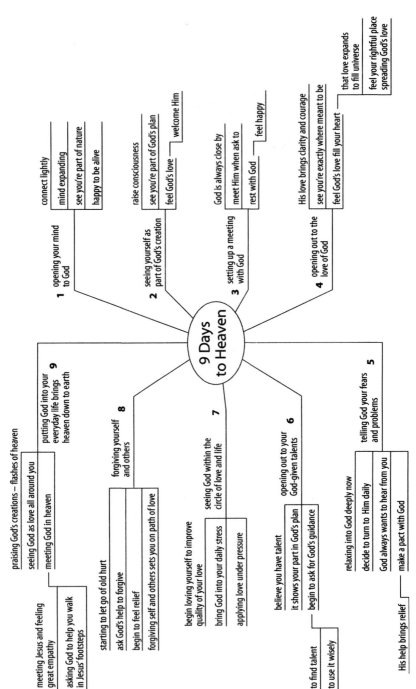

9 Days to Heaven

1 opening your mind to God
- connect lightly
- mind expanding
- see you're part of nature
- happy to be alive

2 seeing yourself as part of God's creation
- raise consciousness
- see you're part of God's plan
- feel God's love — welcome Him

3 setting up a meeting with God
- God is always close by
- meet Him when ask to
- rest with God — feel happy

4 opening out to the love of God
- His love brings clarity and courage
- see you're exactly where meant to be
- feel God's love fill your heart
  - that love expands to fill universe
  - feel your rightful place spreading God's love

5 telling God your fears and problems
- relaxing into God deeply now
- decide to turn to Him daily
- God always wants to hear from you
  - make a pact with God — His help brings relief

6 opening out to your God-given talents
- believe you have talent
- it shows your part in God's plan
- begin to ask for God's guidance
  - to find talent
  - to use it wisely

7 seeing God within the circle of love and life
- begin loving yourself to improve quality of your love
- bring God into your daily stress
- applying love under pressure

8 forgiving yourself and others
- starting to let go of old hurt
- ask God's help to forgive
- begin to feel relief
- forgiving self and others sets you on path of love

9 putting God into your everyday life brings heaven down to earth
- praising God's creations – flashes of heaven
- seeing God as love all around you
- meeting God in heaven
  - meeting Jesus and feeling great empathy
  - asking God to help you walk in Jesus' footsteps

SECTION TWO

The Next Steps

Your prayers

Over the last nine days you have used the following simple prayers to take you closer to God. You may like to commit these to memory.

Perhaps you could write them on small cards and either carry them around with you, or put them in a prominent place in your home. Look at them regularly and say them out loud to keep you focused on God and your goal of heaven.

Day One

Whenever you see a bird in flight remind yourself that you too are playing your own special role in the natural order of life.

Then say the sentence: *'Dear God, I am happy just to be alive,'* and remember the special feeling of love you have experienced.

Day Two

Whenever you see a mountain remind yourself that the mountain, the Universe, the world and you have been designed and created by God through love.

Then say the sentence: *'Dear God, you are welcome, I want you in my life,'* and remember the light and the vibrations of love He brought you.

Day Three

Whenever you see a tree remind yourself that God is always there for you.

Then say the sentence: *'Dear God, I am happy to know you,'* and remember the feeling of peace and tranquillity that His presence gave you.

Day Four

Whenever you see a lit candle remind yourself that God is love.

Then say the sentence: *'Dear God, please guide me every day of my life in the ways to send your love out to others,'* and remember that you have been born for this.

Day Five

Whenever you see running water remind yourself that God wants you to call on Him when you need something.

Then say the sentence: *'Dear God, whenever I have a problem please guide me to the solution,'* and remember the feeling of relief you had when you understood that you are never alone with your problems.

Day Six

Whenever you see a beach remind yourself that you are special and unique.

Then say the sentence: *'Dear God, please show me my talents and how to use them wisely,'* and begin to watch carefully for His clues and guidance.

Day Seven

Whenever you are being jostled in a crowd, remind yourself that whenever you send out love, it increases the supply of love within you.

Then say the sentence: *'Dear God, please remind me to be this loving way at the most stressful times in my life,'* and choose to smile at the strangers instead of scowling.

Day Eight

Whenever you see a rainbow remind yourself that God will always give you the strength to forgive.

Then say the sentence: *'Dear God, please walk along this path of love with me all the days of my life,'* and remember that forgiving yourself and others frees you to live your life fully.

Day Nine

Whenever you see some flowers remind yourself that God and Jesus and heaven are always close by.

Then say the sentence: *'Dear God, please help me to follow the footsteps of Jesus to heaven,'* and remember the air charged with love when you met together in Paradise.

Other prayers

The perfect prayer and the world's most loved is the Lord's Prayer. This is a direct quote of Jesus' words.*

The Lord's Prayer

(You may be familiar with slightly different wording.)

> Our Father who art in heaven,
> Hallowed be Thy name.
> Thy kingdom come,
> Thy will be done,
> On earth as it is in heaven.
> Give us this day our daily bread;
> And forgive us our trespasses,
> As we forgive those who trespass against us;
> And lead us not into temptation,
> But deliver us from evil.

After that the usual response is: Amen. Meaning: let it be so.

A closer look at The Lord's Prayer

This prayer was given to the followers of Jesus in response to

---

*The Lord's Prayer comes from the *Holy Bible*, the New Testament, Matthew chapter 6, verses 9 to 13. Sometimes abbreviated to: Mt 6:9-13. There have been numerous scholarly translations of the original Biblical texts so you may be familiar with another version of the prayer. I have used the one which I have prayed all of my life.

the request – 'Lord, teach us how to pray.' We can therefore be sure that it is the ideal prayer. Spending a few minutes to examine it can reveal a lot, such as the way God wants us to treat Him. And also what He wants from us.

'Our Father, who art in heaven,'

This is specific. It addresses our words directly to God – whilst giving Him the loving title of Father – and opens a channel of communication between us and Him.

You can use this as a reminder to make your requests specifically to God. Not just presume that as He knows your heart and mind He will automatically give His assistance.

As you become used to having God in your life it is easy to begin to take Him for granted. As you have already learnt, God will give His help freely. However, He needs to be asked personally! This is a step that people often miss out and then start to view God through jaundiced eyes.

'Hallowed be Thy name.'

A word of praise for the 'Great Creator'. An acknowledgement of who and what He is.

Every single thing on earth, including all of our possessions, is from God. Have you ever thought about that? The clothes you wear are woven from the cotton He sent. The main component of your computer is a silicone chip made of heated, melted God-given sand. The key you open your door with is of mined, God-made metal. You name it – your food, water, electricity, the paper of this book, everything is from God. It's good to remember that, often.

'Thy Kingdom come, Thy will be done, on earth as it is in heaven.'

This means that we need to be open to whatever God wants for, or of us.

So, when you ask God for something, you also need to acknowledge that it may not be what He wants for you. Yet you can be sure that God has heard your request and will deal with it in His own way.

That being the case you can make a conscious decision to let the problem drop away for some time and leave it in God's hands. 'Let go, and let God,' sums this up.

'Give us this day our daily bread;'

This is asking for God to please let us have the means to continue living in this body on earth. Nothing can be presumed, ever.

This is also a reminder that God sends enough food for everyone on earth to be well fed. We all know that in some parts of the world people are starving. Try regarding this in the new light of your recent experiences, understanding that everything is an opportunity to love. Then, do what you personally can to alleviate suffering through the ballot box, donations, prayers, and other efforts.

'And forgive us our trespasses, as we forgive those who trespass against us;'

This is asking for forgiveness when we are not loving in any situation; in just the same way as we forgive those who are not loving to us in any situation.

Ouch! We are asking God to treat us in exactly the same way as we treat others! That can be your *greatest reminder* to be loving as often as possible.

'Lead us not into temptation, But deliver us from evil.'

When we choose the path of love we will be tempted away from it. Jesus was tempted by evil too.

In our lives, that evil presence can be recognised each and every time we are 'tempted' to go against what we know to be the loving way in any situation.

For example, you buy someone a present knowing they will love it, then you start thinking you could keep it for yourself. Or, you volunteer to help someone out then start getting cold feet about it and try to think of ways to back out of your promise. Or, you want to carry out a familiarisation in the programme but start making excuses to yourself about why you can't do it after all.

Twice a day at least, perhaps in the morning when you wake, or before you go to sleep at night, it's a good idea to use the Lord's Prayer before you begin to have your chat with God.

Throughout the day though, try to speak to God often about anything that you are doing, or going through, just as you do during the programme.

Try building on what you have been doing already by adding in the something like:

- 'Hello God, I'm finding this piece of work very difficult. Will you please help me to get some clarity on it? Thank you.'

- 'Hello God, I'd love to spend a few minutes of my lunch break with you today. Will you please remind me? Thank you.'

- 'Hi God, I feel very irritable this evening. Will you please help me not to take it out on others? Thank you.'

- 'Dear God, will you please help me to see that every problem in my life is an opportunity for me to grow in love? And guide me to the lesson? Thank you.'

You will surely also find inspiration in some of the many beautiful prayers that have been written over the ages. You may like to seek out a book of prayers. (One such volume is 1000 World Prayers by Marcus Braybrooke published by John Hunt Publishing Ltd.)

You can pray to the Queen of Heaven

Many people also pray to Jesus' mother, Mary – sometimes called, Queen of Heaven. Especially when they have problems in their family. They use their own words, or special prayers. The most widely used formal prayer is the Hail Mary:

> Hail Mary, full of grace, the Lord is with thee. Blessed art thou among women. And blessed is the fruit of thy womb, Jesus. Holy Mary, mother of God, pray for us sinners now, and at the hour of our death. Amen.
> (This is based on the Holy Bible, Luke 1:41-42)

This prayer is also used specifically to pray for peace in the world. ('Queen of Peace' is another of Mary's many titles.) This is often done using a rosary. A special string of beads which keeps track of the numbers of prayers said.

When you pray the Hail Mary or rosary on a sunny day you may like to look up at the sky and imagine that the blue is the hem of Mary's cloak. And feel her close to you.

There are many specific prayers

You will discover that there are prayers for many different occasions and circumstances, such as:

- Morning prayers where you might thank God that you woke up and for giving you the gift of a new day.

- Evening prayers where you might thank God for the blessings of your day.

- Prayers to praise God and Jesus for all their blessings and love.

- Prayers for special intentions, which could be anything from the hope for the restoration of the good health of a loved one, to the hope of passing an important exam.

Remember, God wants to hear from you often, no matter what words you use.

Identifying God's guiding hand in your life –
God chooses many ways to contact us

When you pray for guidance of some sort it is important to be aware that in addition to talking to you directly God may use some other means to make contact. The relevant expression is – 'If God doesn't come, He sends.'

Tip: When you ask for guidance, tag on the request for God to make it as clear as possible when the signs appear. These could come from anywhere.

Say, for instance, you have prayed about a major dilemma. You may then be guided by a strong urge to speak about it to someone you hadn't considered. Maybe even a complete stranger.

During the resulting conversation a number of things may happen. The person could:

Supply the answer you were seeking.

Or:

Provide the key to the next step

Or:

Give you some comfort and support through understanding and empathy, which encourages you to keep going until the answer appears.

Other sources of the missing answer could be supplied by, say: a film plot, that just fits your situation; a card on a notice board that you don't know why you looked at, but felt you should; a chance remark by a colleague; a Sunday sermon in church where it seems that the message is specifically for you; an article in a magazine you are flicking through at the dentist; and so on ...

Many people pray for guidance and then dip into their Bible at random seeking the answer. Sometimes it works. Other times it doesn't. God will send the answer in His way.

> *When you ask for God's guidance also request that He make His answer clear*

God's ways hold many pleasant surprises

As your communication with God deepens, some of His ways may surprise you. Such as His sense of humour. Not for nothing is He sometimes referred to as the World's Greatest Comedian.

That too is a lesson. Life can hold many troubles. However, a lot of situations we class as problems are, in reality, only soap operas that we turn into dramas. But we are too closely involved to see it. And the pain we feel is very real.

Try remembering the soap opera angle and applying it where possible. Your absurdity may well make you laugh through your tears, anger, or frustrations. You can be sure that God will be laughing along with you. Never *at* you.

> *When you spot a soap opera drama in your life share a chuckle with God*

Reading the Bible
Through reading the word of God
you come to know His ways

The best place to educate yourself about God and His ways, is to read the Bible. It is the word of God. Often referred to as 'The Greatest Story Ever Told' it speaks of love, miracles, angels, jealousy, treachery, and ultimate triumph over evil.

The Bible, the most widely read book on earth, covers the whole spectrum of human experience. Within its pages is everything you need to know about life and how God wants you to live it. It also contains sound, practical advice that is as valid today as when it was written; human nature is the same now as it always has been.

Little wonder then that the Bible is the world's most complete source of inspiration, motivation and self-help.

The Bible holds all the answers

Look for a Bible that is small enough to be carried around. Many have little line drawings and maps that make the text more understandable.

There are also books available that explain the Bible text in a very simple way. These are a very useful learning tool to deepen your understanding of the original text. (For example, Mark Water's marvellous *Bible Made Easy* series published by John Hunt Publishing Ltd. is most helpful.)

You don't need to put off reading your Bible until you have a big wedge of time at your disposal. Even five minutes is enough to be of benefit, to learn something. When you do have more time though quiet study will bring even more rewards.

Too busy to read your Bible? Just read a few sentences and think about them during your day

The Bible divides into two distinct parts – the Old Testament and the New Testament. It is best to read the New Testament first as it is shorter and simpler to read than the Old Testament. Therefore, as your relationship with God develops, you will find it easier to read the Old Testament too.

The New Testament

The New Testament is a record of the life, teachings and works of Jesus Christ, the Saviour of the world. (The Messiah foretold by God through the prophets in The Old Testament.) It documents His birth, mission on earth, death, resurrection from the dead, and ascension into heaven. And the spread of Christianity by His followers.

The name 'New Testament' means that it is a record of God's new covenant with His people. This covenant, agreement, is the good news that God has promised to save those who believe in Jesus as Lord and Saviour.

Jesus, one part of the Holy Trinity – Father, Son and Holy Spirit – came from His heavenly kingdom to earth to show us the way to everlasting life. From around the age of thirty, He began a mission of about three years during which He preached the good news about God's mercy and the way to heaven and performed countless miracles. His mission on earth culminated in His taking the sins of the whole world, including yours and mine, onto His shoulders. Then, by being nailed to a cross, dying to redeem us from those sins.

Three days later the world's greatest miracle occurred – Jesus rose from the dead. After that the gates of heaven were swung open so that we could enter in.

We can enter heaven because Jesus died to save us

Jesus is still alive and living in heaven. Along with God and the Holy Spirit – it is through the actions of the Holy Spirit that we are able to be in close communion with God and Jesus – He also, is always with you. And will make His presence felt if you ask Him to.

God has asked you to listen to His beloved son. In the New Testament Jesus tells us emphatically, 'I am the Way, the Truth and the Life. No one can come to the Father except through me.' (John 14:6). His message is clear. He is stating that only through following the example and teachings He gave us can we take our lasting place in heaven.

Jesus is the Way to heaven

Jesus, as God-made-man, was subjected to the same human tests that we are. So you can know that He understands your pain. Remember that empathy you felt when He held your hand in His.

So, no matter what situations crop up in your life, you can always find the path of love by reading Jesus' words in the New Testament, following His instructions, and praying for guidance on the best way to do that.

When you read the New Testament you may also like to look out for the following points:

1. Jesus taught that the two chief commandments are: to love God with all your heart, soul, mind and strength; and to love your neighbour as you love yourself (Mark

12:29-31). Then He gave us a new commandment – to love one another just as He had loved us (John 13:34).

That new commandment sums up the essence of all the ten commandments given by God to Moses. Love is the answer in every situation as you have been reminded in the programme. We need to keep reinforcing our chosen path of love. The human brain needs constant reminders to keep it on track.

2. Jesus voluntarily died an agonising, cruel death on the cross for you so that you could have everlasting life with God in heaven (Acts 2:22-36).

   Let the Cross – represented by a crucifix – have a prominent place in your life. For instance, you could put one on a wall in your house; hang a small one on a chain around your neck; put one in your car, and so on as a reminder of His great sacrifice and abiding love for you. It is the purest example of unconditional love the world has ever known.

3. Jesus has said that He is the one who will raise you up into eternal life (John 6:40).

   It is therefore, crucial that you learn as much about Him as possible so that you can follow closely in His footsteps.

4. Jesus wants you to love your enemies and pray for them. He reasoned that anyone can love someone who loves us (Luke 6:27-32).

   Therefore, one of your greatest tests of all is to apply love in the most difficult of circumstances.

5. Jesus said that He will help you with the heavy burdens in your life and promises that in Him you will find rest (Matthew 11:25-28).

So, do remember to call on Him when things get too tough.

6. Jesus was tempted by evil but did not give in to it (Matthew 4:1-10). He told us what to do when we are tempted (Matthew 18:8).

   When you choose for God, Jesus and love, you must expect to be tempted to turn away from them, often. Keep in mind that the force of evil will present itself in a variety of ways and strengths.

   A quick word with God or Jesus will generally help you resist. Sometimes though, longer periods of prayer alone will be needed.

7. Jesus said that you should have faith in God and when you pray for something you need to trust that you will get it (Mark 11:22-25).

   The formula set out in those verses is the basis of the 'affirmations' in this book. It is the most effective way to pray.

   Remember though, that God will not always answer your prayers in the way you expect. However, He will *always* answer. And we must trust Him that everything is working together for good (Romans 8:28).

8. One of Jesus' most famous teaching sessions is the Sermon on the Mount (Matthew 5-7). It is the source of much advice on how to live your life to the full.

   Reading it for the first time you are sure to be amazed that you are so familiar with many of the pearls of wisdom it contains. Indeed, it forms the basis of many of the self-development principles that are so very popular today. For example, live in the *now*. (The rest of the Bible contains the majority of the other wise things we know and read elsewhere, never learning the true source.)

9. Jesus has told us that He will come here again to establish God's Kingdom on earth. And warns that you should watch for the signs that will tell you when this will happen (Luke 21:25-31).

Jesus wants you to be prepared for His second coming by remaining close to Him and God at all times and doing what He asks you to do: grow in love.

Reading The New Testament will bring you closer to God and Jesus through the power of the Holy Spirit.

As mentioned previously many people use their Bibles to dip into for an answer to a specific problem. You may like to do that too sometimes. However, before you start dipping try to read it through at least once.

You could symbolise the importance of the act of reading your Bible by saying a little prayer before you open it each time. Something like, *'Dear God and Jesus, please send your Holy Spirit to help me understand the messages you are trying to pass on to me within these pages.'*

When a verse leaps out at you, you could write it down and carry it around with you. Try to look at it often thinking about its meaning. Try to commit it to memory too. And ask God to show you how to apply its message in your life.

When you have finished reading you could pray, *'Thank you God, Jesus, and Holy Spirit for your help. Please show me how I can put what you ask of me into action in my daily life.'*

When you feel ready, take time to read the Old Testament too.

The Old Testament

This is, amongst other things, the record of God's interactions with nations and individuals from the start of creation. As you become familiar with its contents, God's character, awesome power, and tender love shine out from its pages.

The name Old Testament means that it is a record of God's first covenant with His chosen people.

As you read the Old Testament watch out for the nine points below and discover for yourself the ways in which God demonstrates His nature. The message of many of them is repeated in a variety of situations too numerous to list.

1. God is your rock and your fortress in times of distress (2 Samuel 22:2-4).

Remember to keep turning to God first when you are in trouble. He will always be there for you.

2. You may go through some bad times but Joy will always follow this (Psalms 30).

When you are going through testing times keep praying and putting yourself into God's hands and you will come through.

3. God is your shepherd and will always lead you along the right path when you ask Him to (Psalms 23).

Remember to call on God whenever you need guidance, and to be specific.

4. God gave us Ten Commandments (Exodus 20), which show us exactly what He expects of us as we go through life.

After reading them over you might like to write them down and look at them often. And commit them to memory.

5. God is full of tenderness and compassion (Exodus 34:6).
   Try as much as you possibly can to follow His lead as you interact with people each day.

6. God is always close to you, however, as the Creator of all, many of His ways are too mysterious to understand (Job 38-41).
   If, for a time, things seem to go badly wrong, you might well find the word 'Why?' rising up. Reading over even part of chapters 38-41 of the book of Job could really help you to put things into perspective. After that try to put yourself back into God's hands and keep trusting.

7. If you fall into bad ways and then have sincere regrets and turn back to God again He will show you mercy (Jonah 3:10).
   At some time you may be so tempted by evil that you turn away from your path of love. But as soon as you have understood that that is what has happened, try to pray to God immediately and ask for His forgiveness.
   And when you have got that, try to let it be a reminder to be as forgiving with others as God is with you.

8. God so loved the world that He sent us His only Son to be our Saviour, Messiah, after repeatedly foretelling this through His prophets (Isaiah 61:1–2). He wants us to know Him through Jesus.
   When Jesus began his public ministry he went into

the Temple, and by using the above reading of Isaiah proclaimed that He was indeed the one whom God had sent, that Messiah (Luke 4:16-21).

Try to remember God's tremendous love for us in sending Jesus to us to show us the way to heaven. And remember too, to do what He asks of you.

9. God rested on the seventh day of Creation (Exodus 31:17).

God has asked you to do the same by making Sunday a Holy Day (the root of the word 'holiday'). First of all God wants you to spend time with Him. Then He wants you to take some relaxation for yourself to recharge your batteries for the new week ahead.

This is such a logical thing to ask. You know that unless you make a definite punctuation between one week and the next you soon become crazy and exhausted, as your life seems to run away with itself.

Making the effort to apply the above nine points in your daily life will take you nearer to God as you are doing what He asks of you.

Attending a church service

Spending time with like-minded people keeps the goal of heaven fixed in mind

In addition to spending regular quality time with God and Jesus, private prayer, reading the Bible, and being loving, Christians are asked to make a further commitment to their pursuit of heaven by regularly meeting together to worship with other Christians. This is done during a church service.

If you need any more incentive, *Time Magazine*, June 1996, reported that various medical studies have shown that regularly attending church services can: lower blood pressure; half the risk of dying from coronary heart disease, and lower rates of depression. And that regular churchgoers are generally more healthy than non-churchgoers.

Going to church keeps you healthier

It could be that you already belong to a branch of the Church (the capital 'C' denotes the members otherwise referred to as the 'living Church') and either attend services often or occasionally. In which case you may now want to move on to the next section: 'Getting the Most From a Church Service'.

If you follow a faith other than Christian, 'Getting the Most From a Church Service' can also be applied to your own form of worship, so you may want to move on to the second paragraph of that section now.

Maybe, though you do not go to church, you have already been baptised into a particular branch of the Church and your family is following that way to God. In that case it is logical to begin taking part in services of that denomination with them.

If you do not have this ready-made support group, or it holds no appeal for you, pray to God and Jesus for guidance. They will give it freely.

Perhaps you would value more advice on choosing a Church but it is very difficult to do this. The criteria are so diverse and personal and the options too numerous to detail in this little book. For instance, some Churches have services that are quite informal, such as Protestant Evangelical. While others, including the Catholic and Orthodox Churches, are more structured with defined rituals.

Actually, choosing a Church is a book in itself. I have come across such books written on the subject but have none to recommend. This is because the only ones I saw took a highly subjective look and a position of venomous anger at branches of Christianity other than their own. Since they were not following the Commandment to love, I was perplexed about their motives. (I prayed for them and sent them love.)

(The Roman Catholic Church has nourished my soul and spirit the whole of my life and been a great consolation to me through the hardest times. It is leading me to God and Jesus.

I have close friends who belong to other Churches including the Church of England, and Orthodox, or who follow other religious faiths such as Jewish or Muslim. All of these friends are loving people. Anyone else writing this book would, I'm sure, recommend their personal Church or religious path to you. Similarly, the only religious path I want to personally recommend to you is Christianity.

Jesus said emphatically, 'I am the Way; the Truth and the Life. No one can come to the Father except through me.' (John

14:5). I believe this absolutely.

And the only Church I can personally recommend to you is the Catholic Church. It has around one billion members so you will be in good company.)

Try out a number of Churches if you feel guided to. However, caution should be applied. Seek out denominations that are long established and accountable to a higher authority with missions and branches around the world. *Do **not** join a sect.*

Take time to do some research, and Pray, Pray, Pray.

If you don't know anyone from a Church you are guided to try out, get an address and phone number from your local directory and ask for the time of the busiest service on a Sunday. Then go along and just join in.

Getting the most from
a church service

This can be used by Christians or those of other faiths to enhance the quality of their worship

Church services give thanks and praise to God for all His gifts, especially the gift of His Son, Jesus to the world. Jesus asked us to commemorate the creation of God's new and everlasting covenant, which took place during the Last Supper, the night before His Crucifixion. This commemoration generally forms the central focus of the service.

Most words and prayers of these services are direct quotes from the Bible, therefore, they will bring these events that you are reading about alive for you.

Go about fifteen minutes ahead of time. Sit in the middle of the church and spend a few minutes looking around at the building and its contents, even if you are very familiar with it. Then close your eyes, take a deep breath, and after breathing out slowly ask Jesus to sit beside you and be your guide and companion during the service.

Ask Jesus to be your guide during the service

In this way you will get the most out of the experience and it will really feed your soul and spirit. Tell Jesus if there is anyone you know who needs some help – perhaps they are sick or have been bereaved, for instance – and ask for His blessings on them.

Throughout the service always be aware that Jesus is beside you and that you are in His house and He's happy to have you there. Through listening to His words being spoken aloud, you are getting to know Him better.

If the service is new to you, try not to judge the proceedings but instead, keep your heart open and just follow what everyone else does. There may be standing, sitting and even kneeling at certain points. There is a regular order as you will discover every time you visit.

After the service has ended stay where you are for a few more minutes. Sit down, close your eyes, and thank Jesus for His company. Then ask for His blessings on your coming week.

Outside the church, try to have a few words with other members of the congregation. Maybe mention you are a newcomer, and so on.

Make sure to speak to someone after the service

Go back the next Sunday and do exactly the same thing. In the meantime keep doing the familiarisations and visualisations in the programme, speaking to God and Jesus, asking for guidance, and reading your Bible. If at any time you feel that you want extra information or help speak to someone at the church.

When you feel ready you may like to become a permanent member of that Church. This is done by being baptised, or christened as it is otherwise called. Tell whoever you speak to at church that this is your wish and ask them to refer you to the relevant person for details and information on the preparation process.

When you are ready join the Church permanently

Healthy living
Nine practical steps to better health

The body is sometimes referred to as the 'temple of the soul.' Without it you would be unable to experience life on earth. Looking at it from this angle may give you a sense of responsibility to nurture yours.

Take a moment to consider this: the prototype of your body was created many thousands of years ago. It has changed very little since then.

Try to picture the lifestyle of prehistoric man, basic and primitive, wandering from place to place, seeking shelter, warmth, water and food where they could.

Food would have been anything they could pick off trees and bushes – fruit, berries and nuts, as well as roots and succulent leaves that could be foraged.

These foodstuffs were the fuel on which the human body was designed to run.

Don't forget what fuel your body was designed to run on: raw food

Over time our dietary intake has been transformed almost beyond recognition.

Many people eat little, if any, raw food. Preferring instead to cook ingredients, often destroying much of its nutritional value.

Then, add into the equation substances such as coffee, tea, dairy produce, and the dead flesh of animals. Not to mention toxins from pesticides, badly made cooking equipment and drinking vessels, and the very air we breathe.

Phew! Just thinking about all that is enough to send the stress levels soaring. This loads our bodies with even more toxins as the 'fight or flight' instinct of primitive man is activated but the resulting adrenaline not used up. (*See point 4 below for one solution to counteract this.) The same thing happens when we live with guilt or blame at our core.

Little wonder then that the miracle of the body and its functions eventually go into overload – with disease as the result.

This is the point at which many people start to point the finger of blame at God. Not fair!

Your body is a finely-tuned miracle of engineering and needs to be treated as such

So, what can you do to stay healthy or begin to work towards the recovery of good health?

Here is the good news. Those nine experiences of God have already begun to nourish all four aspects of who you are – body, mind, soul and spirit. Tension has been released from all four. If you *feel* good, every part of you works better.

And remember, the added bonus is that you also look better. The flow of love within us always makes us look better on the outside too. When people have mentioned your increasing outward glow since you started this programme I hope you told them that your secret is: God.

Pass on the message that God is your new beauty secret

Nine ways to health

For optimum all-round health, try incorporating the following nine adjustments into your lifestyle. You'll soon notice the difference.

1. Stop criticising yourself – this will immediately make you feel better. Soon you will notice that you have also stopped attracting criticism from others.

2. Daily drink 6–8 glasses of purified water – our bodies are made up of at least 70 per cent water and we need to keep changing it.

3. Daily, eat at least 5 portions of organic fresh fruit or raw vegetables. These will not only provide essential nutrients and fibre they will also reduce cravings for highly processed foods.

4. Do a 20-minute stint of non-stop gentle exercise , for example, a brisk walk, swimming , dancing or cycling, a few times a week.
    *This is especially important to combat stress toxicity. It will pep up your metabolism and help to burn off calories faster too. (Consult a doctor before embarking upon any new exercise programme.)

5. Cut down on alcohol intake and reduce or stop smoking. Both can negatively affect your body and life. You may need to mentally prepare yourself for a while. When you are ready – do it and pray for help.

6. At least once a week take a walk in nature in say, a park, the countryside, a beach, or beside a river. This will automatically quieten your mind and bring you in tune with God.

7. Weekly buy some fresh flowers and make a point of looking at them often and praising God for his amazing work. This will lift your spirits and also boost your lymphatic system.

8. Practise unconditional love for self, others and God. When you learn to love yourself well by accepting exactly who you are, faults and all, and treating yourself kindly at all times you will be able to start loving others and God in the same way.

9. Daily do something for someone else. This could be giving major help. Or something as simple as say, calling a friend with a bit of encouragement when you know they are feeling low.

Looking your best!
Feeling marvellous!

Conclusion

This simple programme has facilitated your recent experiences of God, Jesus and heaven. The following nine highlighted points from it will keep your eyes lovingly fixed on your heavenly goal.

At a glance – how to keep facing your goal:

1. **Make regular time-slots to be alone with God.**
   All relationships need nurturing. Never be too busy to spend some quality time with God.

2. **Speak to God frequently throughout every day.**
   When you keep God at the front of your mind your life will stay in balance.

3. **When you want God's help or guidance – ask!**
   Never assume that because God loves you and knows what you want and need He will automatically drop gifts into your lap. God will work with you, not for you!

4. **Remind yourself that you are being tested daily by evil to try to get you to turn away from God.**
   Always be on guard to defend and protect your relationship with God. Speak God's name and He will be beside you, instantly. Reading God's word, the Bible, will keep you strong and feed your soul.

5. Regularly seek out people walking on the road to love as you are.

Try to cultivate friendships with godly, loving people. Those who live their lives in ways that inspire you to keep on with your goal of God and heaven.

Your family and old friends will benefit from your growing love; if they want to.

6. Listen and watch out for God's guidance at all times.

God is guiding your life because you have asked Him to do so.

When you recognise His lessons and assistance remember to thank Him. Never take God for granted.

7. Regularly look for ways to help others.

Love grows through being given away. Being selfless will anchor your feet firmly on the road towards God and heaven.

8. Seek out quiet, natural surroundings as often as possible.

Nature will soothe you and bring you back to your glorious humanity as you remember you are in perfect harmony with it.

9. Pass on the message of God and Jesus and their love.

When you feel ready gently begin to speak about your experiences with God and Jesus to those you feel are open to receive the information. These may be family, friends, or strangers. You will surely recognise their unfulfilled yearning.

Before you begin to speak, remember to pray for guidance and the Holy Spirit will help you.

MAY GOD CONTINUE TO BLESS YOU ALWAYS!